We the People

Civic Values in America

Kelly Rodgers

Consultant

Caryn Williams, M.S.Ed.
Madison County Schools
Huntsville, AL

Image Credits: Cover & p.1 Ariel Skelley/age fotostock; p.13 (bottom) Blend Images/Alamy; p.9 (bottom) Buyenlarge/Getty Images; p.24 Catchlight Visual Services/Alamy; p.27 JSP Studios/Alamy; pp.2–3, 26 Richard Levine/Alamy; p.8, 14–15 The Bridgeman Art; p.25 (middle) Dan Porges/Getty Images; p.4 (middle bottom) Stock Montage/Getty Images; p.21 The Granger Collection, NYC/The Granger Collection; pp.3, 6 (bottom), 7 (top), 18, 22, 23 (top), 25 (top), 32 iStock; p.4 (middle top) LOC, LC-DIG-pga-01602; p.20 LOC, LC-DIG-pga-01767; p.4 (left bottom) LOC, LC-DIG-ppmsca-17523; p.4 (right bottom) LOC, LC-DIG-ppmsca-24329; p.5 (middle bottom) LOC, LC-DIG-ppmsca-31158; p.19 LOC, LC-DIG-ppmsca-37242; p.4 (right top) LOC, LC-USZC2-3273; p.15 LOC, LC-USZ62-59464 The Library of Congress; p.23 (left bottom) Jim Pickerell Stock Connection Worldwide/Newscom; pp.9 (top), 10–13 North Wind Picture Archives; p.15 Getty Images/SuperStock; p.9 (background) US National Archives; pp.4 (left top), 5 (middle top, left top, left bottom, right top & bottom), 7 (both bottom), 12 (left), 17 (all), Wikimedia Commons; all other images from Shutterstock.

Teacher Created Materials

5301 Oceanus Drive
Huntington Beach, CA 92649-1030
http://www.tcmpub.com

ISBN 978-1-4333-7366-4

© 2015 Teacher Created Materials, Inc.

Table of Contents

American Values 4

A New Nation 8

All Are Created Equal 10

The Law of the Land 14

Responsible Citizens 22

We the People 27

Blog It! 28

Glossary 30

Index 31

Your Turn! 32

American Values

Being an American is not about your skin color, the clothes you wear, or how you look. So what does it mean to be an American? America's past can help us find the answer. Early American leaders built our country on certain **values**. They wrote about these important values in the **U.S. Constitution** (kon-sti-TOO-shuhn).

Early American Leaders

There were many early leaders who helped make America what it is today.

Patrick Henry

George Washington

Martha Washington

Alexander Hamilton

Dolley Madison

James Madison

Our early leaders wrote that Americans should be free. They thought that Americans should believe what they want to believe, and say what they want to say. Americans should feel safe and be happy. The leaders said that Americans should be treated fairly. They stated that people should not be allowed to hurt one another. They also thought that they should be able to choose their leaders. These are **rights** that all Americans have. These ideas and rights are still important to Americans. We call them our **civic** values.

John Adams

Abigail Adams

Samuel Adams

Benjamin Franklin

Thomas Jefferson

Mercy Otis Warren

We get to enjoy many rights in America. But being an American is not just about the rights we have. It is also about being a good **citizen**. Good citizens have **responsibilities** (ri-spon-suh-BIL-i-teez). These are duties that we should do.

You have duties in your home. It may be your duty to clean the dishes or to keep your room clean. You also have duties in school. It is your duty to learn and to be nice to others.

These kids are being good citizens by cleaning up their community.

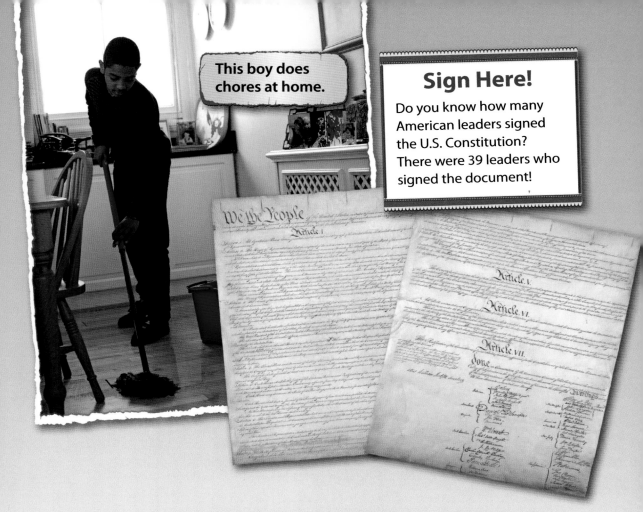

This boy does chores at home.

Sign Here!

Do you know how many American leaders signed the U.S. Constitution? There were 39 leaders who signed the document!

We all have responsibilities to our country, too. It is our duty to follow the rules and laws. It is our duty to treat others fairly. The U.S. Constitution lists these rights and responsibilities. It talks about America's values.

The U.S. Constitution is proof that our country is built on these values. America's early leaders set an example for us. They worked hard, and they relied on themselves. They helped make America what it is today. It is up to us to follow their example.

A New Nation

In the 1600s, people left Great Britain to live in America. They came for many reasons. Some wanted freedom to practice their religion. They were called *Puritans*.

By 1776, many more people from Europe were living in America. They were living in the 13 **colonies**. Great Britain and its king controlled these colonies. The **colonists** felt that the king was not treating them fairly. They wanted to be free from his rule. They wanted their own country.

The leaders in the colonies got together and wrote the Declaration of **Independence** (in-di-PEN-duhns). It was a letter to the king. It said that the colonies were now free from British rule and they would start a new country. But the king wanted to keep the colonies. This started a war. In 1783, the colonists won the war, and a new nation was born. It was called the United States of America.

George Washington leads the American army.

Puritans land in Plymouth, Massachusetts in 1620.

American Indian Values

American Indians were living in America long before the Puritans. They had important values, too. Family was very important to early American Indians. They also had great respect for the land.

American Indian family in 1899

9

All Are Created Equal

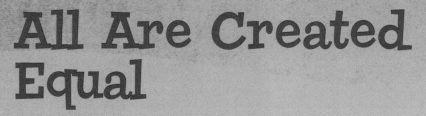

The Declaration of Independence did more than say that the colonies were free. It said what kind of nation America would be. It said that the people would be in charge of the country. It said that the people had certain rights.

Thomas Jefferson was one of the early leaders in America. He helped write the Declaration. His words explained the beliefs of the new nation. Jefferson wrote, "All men are created equal." Our values are based on this idea.

Helping Hands

Four men helped Jefferson write the Declaration of Independence: John Adams, Benjamin Franklin, Robert Livingston, and Roger Sherman.

But Americans did not treat all people the same. In Jefferson's time, many people were slaves. Slaves had no freedom. Other people owned them. Women did not have the same rights as white men either. Jefferson's promise of **equality** was a good idea. But future Americans would have to work hard to make this promise come true. Today, we continue to work toward equality for all people.

These slaves are forced to harvest sugar cane long ago.

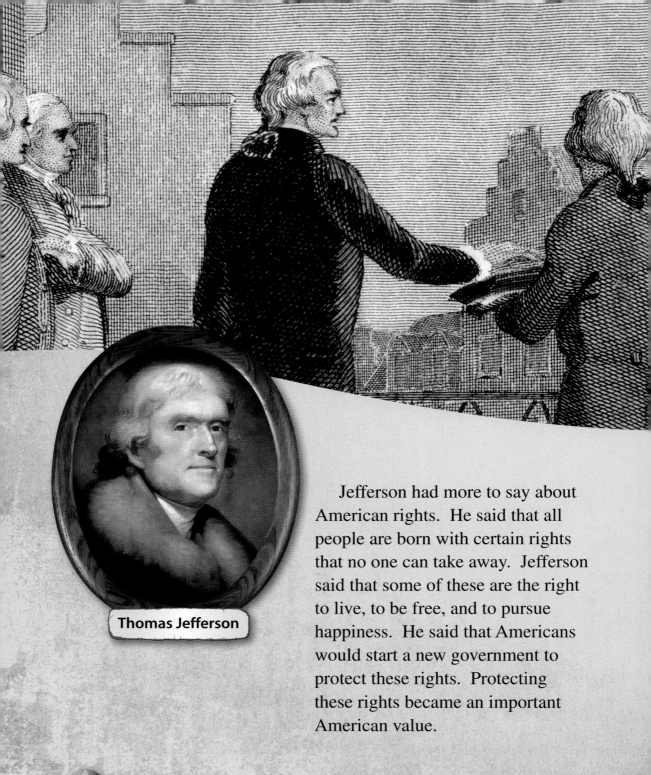

Thomas Jefferson

Jefferson had more to say about American rights. He said that all people are born with certain rights that no one can take away. Jefferson said that some of these are the right to live, to be free, and to pursue happiness. He said that Americans would start a new government to protect these rights. Protecting these rights became an important American value.

George Washington is sworn in as the president in 1789.

Jefferson also said that the people should choose their leaders. One person should not have all the power. He did not want another king to rule America. Jefferson said that if the people did not get to choose their leaders, the government would not be fair. This idea is known as "the consent of the governed." This means that people should agree on who their leaders are. It became another civic value. This is why we vote for, or choose, our leaders.

The Law of the Land

In 1777, American leaders wrote a constitution. It said how the government should work. It stated the rules and laws of the nation. Many Americans did not want a strong government. This reminded them of the British king. They wanted the people to have the power. This first constitution was called the **Articles of Confederation** (kuhn-fed-uh-REY-shuhn). But there were problems with the Articles. The government was not strong enough to keep the new nation safe.

George Washington speaks at the Constitutional Convention, 1787.

ARTICLES
OF
CONFEDERATION
AND
PERPETUAL UNION
BETWEEN THE
STATES
OF

NEW-HAMPSHIRE, MASSACHUSETTS-BAY, RHODE-ISLAND AND PROVIDENCE PLANTATIONS, CON-NECTICUT, NEW-YORK, NEW-JERSEY, PENNSYL-VANIA, DELAWARE, MARYLAND, VIRGINIA, NORTH CAROLINA, SOUTH CAROLINA AND GEOR-GIA.

WILLIAMSBURG:
Printed by J. DIXON & W. HUNTER.
M,DCC,LXXVIII.

The leaders met to write a new constitution. It was a hard job. No other country had tried to form the kind of government that America wanted. Some people thought it would not work. They said it was dangerous to give the people so much power.

In 1789, the U.S. Constitution was ready. It said how we would choose our leaders. It listed our rights and duties. It was based on the values of the people.

One branch of government meets in the U.S. Capitol building.

The new government was created to protect the rights of the people. The U.S. Constitution said that one person would not have all the power. The power would be shared. The states would be in charge of themselves, but there would also be a central government. It would be in charge of the whole country.

The U.S. Constitution has three parts. The preamble is the introduction. It states why the U.S. Constitution was written. It says what "we the people" believe. It says that we value **justice**, or fairness, and peace. It also says that we value freedom.

The articles are the body of the U.S. Constitution. They explain how our government works. Three branches, or parts, share the power. The branches are like legs on a stool. They are separate, but they all work together to make the stool stand.

The **amendments** are the third part. They are changes. They allow the U.S. Constitution to grow and change with our nation.

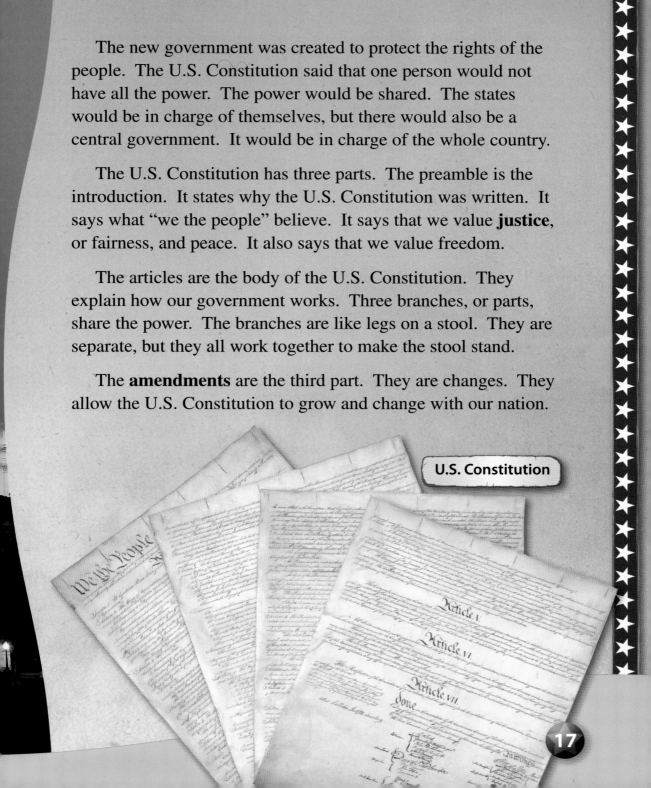

U.S. Constitution

The Bill of Rights

The U.S. Constitution was written to protect our rights. But some people thought that more rights were needed. They wanted all of these rights to be added to the U.S. Constitution. They asked for a Bill of Rights. These became the first 10 amendments to the U.S. Constitution.

The First Amendment protects basic freedoms. It includes freedom of religion. This means that the government cannot make you practice a certain religion. You can believe what you want to believe. It also includes freedom of speech and freedom of the press. This means that you can say what you want to say. You can even speak out against the government!

The Second Amendment protects our right to defend ourselves. Other amendments explain the rights of fair punishment. Many people think that the Bill of Rights is the best statement of our values. It explains what it means to be an American.

These people march for their freedom and rights in 1963.

CRUSADE FOR VOTERS
Savannah Freedom Now Movement . . .
FFILIATED S.C.L.C.

More Amendments

Today, we have many of the same values that our early leaders had. We still think that people should be free. And we still think that all people should be treated fairly. But our ideas about how to live out these values have changed over time. New amendments have been added to solve new problems. These amendments show how America has changed.

In 1865, the Thirteenth Amendment ended slavery. The Fourteenth Amendment says that anyone born in America is a citizen. The Fifteenth Amendment gave all men the right to vote. In 1920, the Nineteenth Amendment gave women the right to vote.

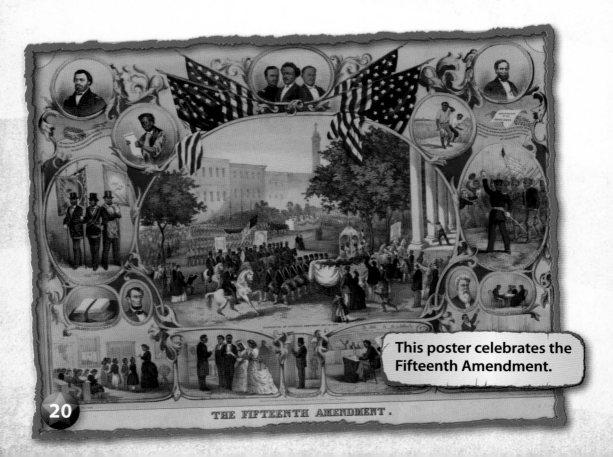

This poster celebrates the Fifteenth Amendment.

THE FIFTEENTH AMENDMENT.

The U.S. Constitution tells us what Americans value. It explains how our government works. Our early leaders worked hard to make a fair government. They wanted a country that would protect its people. They also wanted a country that would grow and change with its people. The amendments are proof of this idea.

Women march for the right to vote in 1912.

Responsible Citizens

With rights come responsibilities. Responsible citizens are good citizens. They work hard to make their country a better place. They follow the rules and laws. They try to do what is best for everyone. They treat others fairly, and they help people in need.

There are other ways to be a good citizen. People can give their time, money, or items to help others. Some people give these things to charities (CHAR-i-teez). These are groups that help people in need. Good citizens can also volunteer. This means they do work that helps others for free.

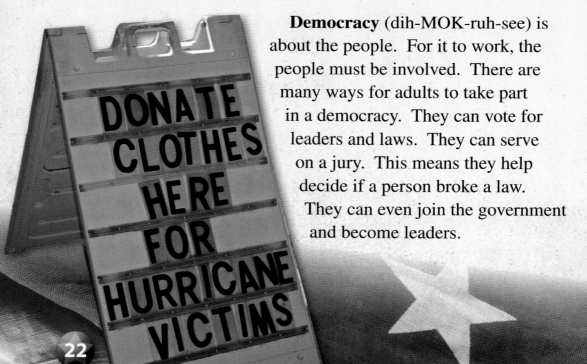

Democracy (dih-MOK-ruh-see) is about the people. For it to work, the people must be involved. There are many ways for adults to take part in a democracy. They can vote for leaders and laws. They can serve on a jury. This means they help decide if a person broke a law. They can even join the government and become leaders.

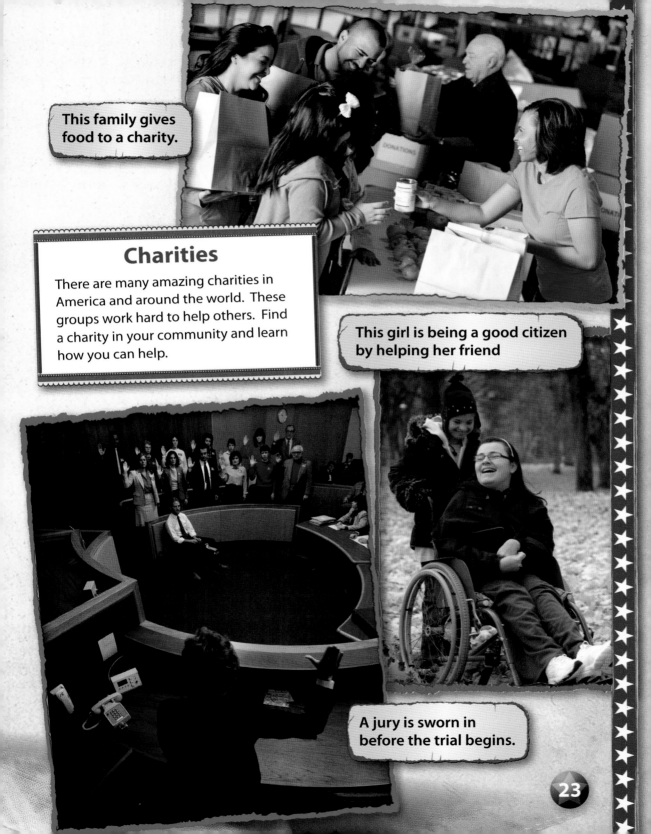

This family gives food to a charity.

Charities

There are many amazing charities in America and around the world. These groups work hard to help others. Find a charity in your community and learn how you can help.

This girl is being a good citizen by helping her friend

A jury is sworn in before the trial begins.

You can be a responsible citizen, too. Follow the rules at home and at school. Do not break our country's laws. Get involved in your community and government. You can learn about your local leaders. You can learn about our country's leaders. You can help keep your community clean and safe. If you see someone being treated unfairly, speak up!

You can donate items to a food bank. You can volunteer at an animal **shelter**. You can pick up trash at a local park. You can be honest and fair. You can be a leader at school and in your home. And you can always work your hardest and do your best. It is never too early to learn how to be a good citizen. Learning to be a responsible citizen is an important American value.

This woman volunteers at an animal shelter.

These people volunteer to build houses for the needy.

Food Banks

Food banks provide free food for people in need. Food banks need volunteers to help sort and box food.

DONATION

These children show their love for America by waving American flags.

We the People

American values come from our past and our present. America's early leaders worked hard to create a country that would support these values. Their ideas are found in the Declaration of Independence. They are also found in the U.S. Constitution. These values tell us what it means to be an American.

We are still learning how to live by these values. As our country changes over time, we will face new problems. So we must find new ways to solve these problems. It is important we make sure that all people still have liberty and justice.

As Americans, we are in charge of our government. We get to choose our own leaders. We also get to vote on our laws. We believe in equality. We think that all people should be treated fairly. The U.S. Constitution protects our rights. To keep these rights, we have responsibilities. We need to be good citizens in order to keep America strong.

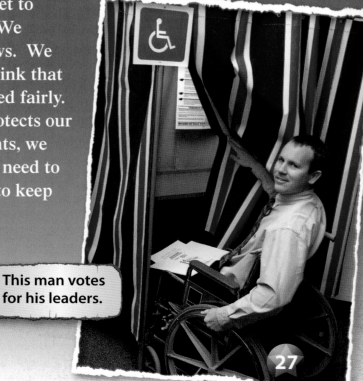

This man votes for his leaders.

Blog It!

Our early leaders worked hard to make America a strong country. They fought a war to be free. They wrote the Constitution to make sure the people had rights and would keep those rights. There have been many great American leaders. Choose one and learn more about him or her. Then, write a blog about that person. Share your blog with others!

This girl learns about George Washington online.

"George Washington was the first president."

This boy writes a blog about an American leader.

These kids look for books on American leaders.

Glossary

amendments—changes to the words or meaning of a law or document

Articles of Confederation—the first set of laws for the United States before the constitution

citizen—a person who legally belongs to a country

civic—having to do with being a citizen

colonies—areas ruled by another country

colonists—people who live in a colony

democracy—a form of government in which people choose leaders by voting

equality—being equal or the same

independence—freedom from outside control or support

justice—fairness

responsibilities—tasks or duties that are required

rights—things a person should be allowed to have or to do

shelter—a place that provides food and protection for people or animals that need help

U.S. Constitution— the system of beliefs and laws by which the United States is organized

values—strongly held beliefs about what is important

Index

Adams, Abigail, 5

Adams, John, 5, 10

Adams, Samuel, 5

American Indians, 9

Articles of Confederation,
    14–15

Bill of Rights, 18

Declaration of Independence,
    8, 10, 27

Franklin, Benjamin, 5, 10

Hamilton, Alexander, 4

Henry, Patrick, 4

Jefferson, Thomas, 5, 10–13

Livingston, Robert, 10

Madison, Dolley, 4

Madison, James, 4

Puritans, 8–9

Sherman, Roger, 10

U.S. Constitution, 4, 7, 15,
    17–18, 21, 27

Warren, Mercy Otis, 5

Washington, George, 4, 8, 13,
    15, 28

Washington, Martha, 4

Your Turn!

Important Values

Think about the American values in this book. Which do you think is the most important value? Why do you think that? Create a poster about the value you choose.